MORE FUN
WITH
SCIENCE

by Derek Dwyer *and* Jill Corby
designed and illustrated by John Lobban

Ladybird Books

ELECTRICITY

Be a bright spark!

Make a circuit

You will need:

Torch battery
Thin plastic-covered wire
Torch bulb

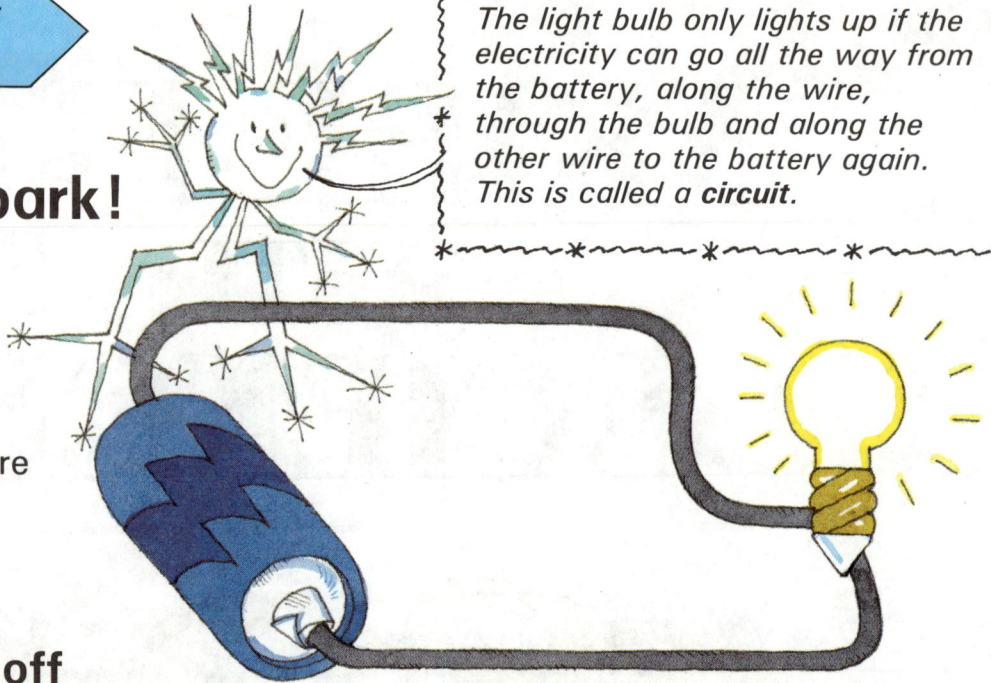

The light bulb only lights up if the electricity can go all the way from the battery, along the wire, through the bulb and along the other wire to the battery again. This is called a **circuit**.

Switching on and off

If you break the circuit on purpose and join it up again you can switch the bulb on and off. Try making a switch.

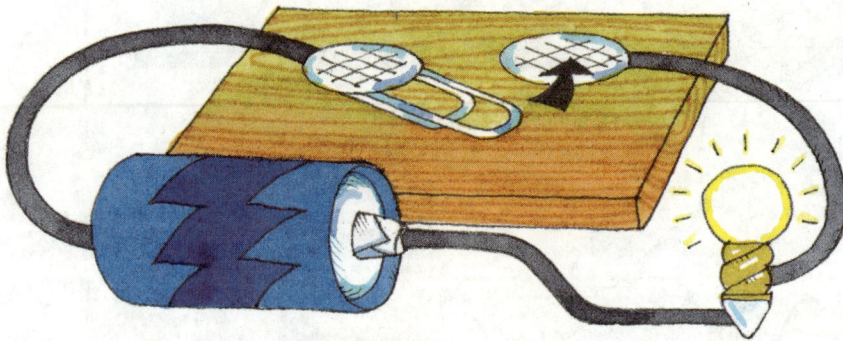

You will need:

Flat piece of wood
Two short nails
Paper clip

Ask a grown-up before you start and don't hit your finger with the hammer!

An electrician's nightmare
Some of these light bulbs are connected into proper circuits. The others are not wired up properly. Can you work out which bulbs should light up and put a tick by those bulbs?

Share and share alike!

We lit two bulbs with one battery. How many bulbs will your battery light?

If you can light more than two, colour the extra bulbs and wires on the picture.

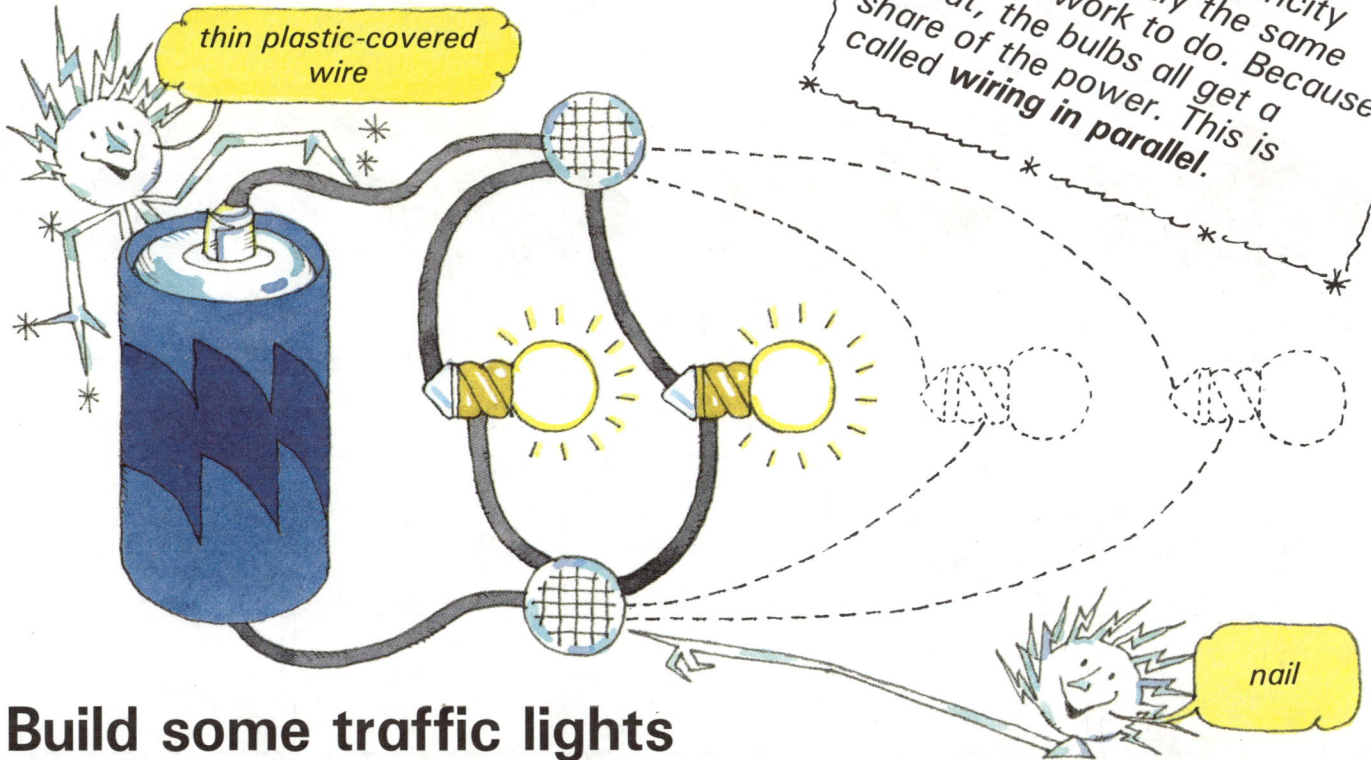

thin plastic-covered wire

nail

Why it works
Electricity always chooses the easiest path. Whichever bulb it goes through, the electricity has almost exactly the same amount of work to do. Because of that, the bulbs all get a share of the power. This is called **wiring in parallel.**

Build some traffic lights

These traffic lights use some of the ideas we've been trying out.

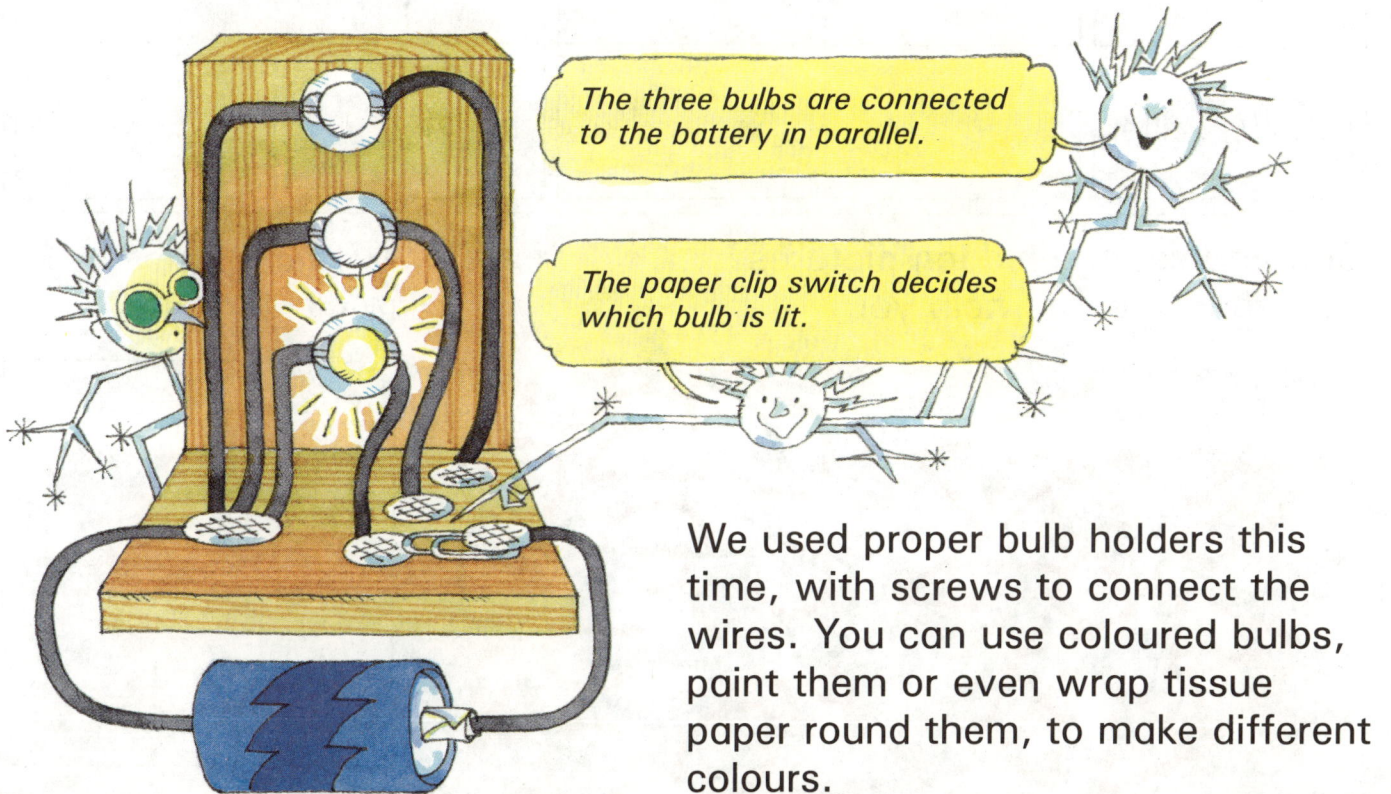

The three bulbs are connected to the battery in parallel.

The paper clip switch decides which bulb is lit.

We used proper bulb holders this time, with screws to connect the wires. You can use coloured bulbs, paint them or even wrap tissue paper round them, to make different colours.

You've got to be bright!

Collect coloured see-through sweet wrappers. Look at lots of different things through them. What do you notice? Materials that stop some colours of light from passing through are called **filters**.

Look at these pictures through your filters.

Record what you saw on this chart.

	Red fish	Yellow fish	Green fish	Blue fish
Red filter	almost disappeared			looked black
yellow filter				
Green filter				
Blue filter				

Can you see the hidden pictures?
Use your filters to help you.

Make a hidden picture like ours.

Light entertainment!

Hold a ruler in a bowl of water. Get down level with it. The ruler isn't really bent. The light from the ruler is bent as it passes from the water into the air.

Now try this. Put a mirror in the water. Lean it against the side of the bowl. Let bright sunlight shine on it through a window. Somewhere nearby there should be a rainbow. Of course it's not really a rainbow because there isn't any rain. It's called a **spectrum**.

Why it works

The light has been bent, just like it was when you looked at the ruler. The colours are all bent by different amounts and that's why they are split up and a rainbow is formed.

The light fantastic

Light travels very fast – nearly 300,000 kilometres every second!

Light from the Sun (our nearest star) gets to us in about eight and a quarter minutes.

After the Sun, the nearest star is called Proxima Centauri. Its light takes almost four and a quarter years to reach us.

Light from the Moon takes just over one and a quarter seconds to get here.

Mirror mirror on the wall...

Can you read these?

ЯOЯЯIM A ƎƧU

∩∩∩‿∩∩∩

Multiplying with mirrors

Tape two mirrors together like a book. Now put something in front of them and quite close. You will see at least two reflections.

By opening or closing the book shape you should be able to make more reflections.

How many can you make?

The mirrors are reflecting the image back to each other again and again.

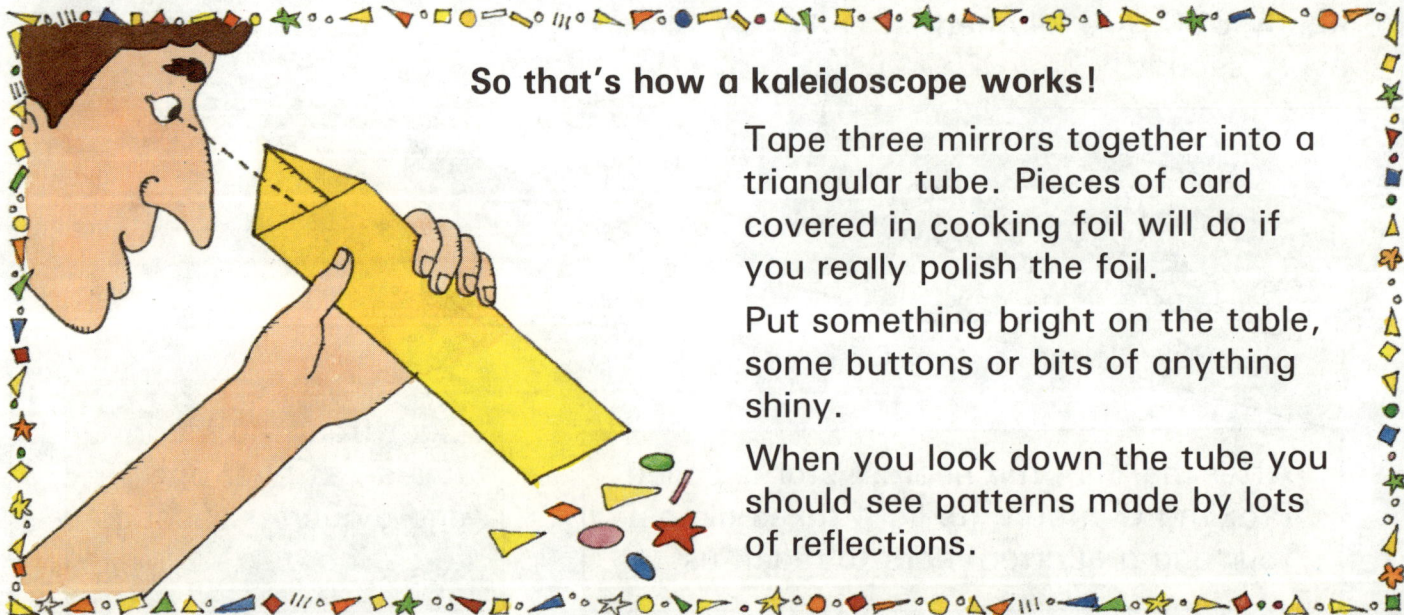

So that's how a kaleidoscope works!

Tape three mirrors together into a triangular tube. Pieces of card covered in cooking foil will do if you really polish the foil.

Put something bright on the table, some buttons or bits of anything shiny.

When you look down the tube you should see patterns made by lots of reflections.

In a flat spin!

The Sun is our nearest star. It is one and a half million times bigger than Earth and is very hot... about 5,500°C! It is 150 million kilometres away.

It would take more than eighty Moons to make another Earth. The Moon is 384,400 kilometres away.

Make a Sun, Moon and Earth mobile

Planet Earth

The Moon

The Sun

Straightened out coathanger wire will do for the beams. Plastic balls are best for the three bodies. Move the places where the threads tie onto the beams until it all hangs level. Now the Moon should turn round (**orbit**) the Earth and they should both **orbit** the Sun.

If you can't find balls the right size, you can make the Sun and planets from card discs with slots, fitted together like this:

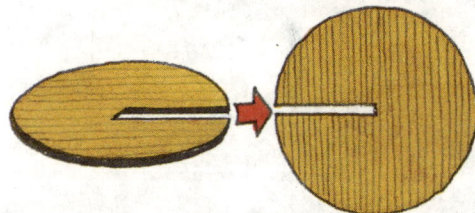

Is it really like that?

No, because you can't get the sizes and distances right in a small model. If the Moon were the size of a golf ball then the Earth would be a small football, four and a half metres away. The Sun would be one and three quarter kilometres away, and bigger than a house!

Moonstruck!

During a **lunar** (Moon) month, the Moon goes through changes called **phases**. As the bright face of the Moon seems to grow we say it **waxes**. When it shrinks we say it **wanes**.

new moon	*waxing*	half moon	*waxing*	full moon

waning	half moon	*waning*	no moon

Can you see the Moon tonight?

Draw it in this square.

Which phase is it in?

Do you think it is waxing (growing bigger) or waning (shrinking)? *Shrinking*

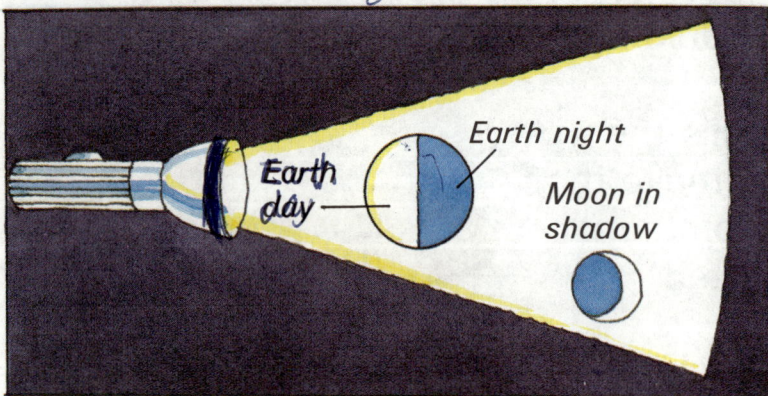

Why does the Moon have phases?

In a dark room, use a torch for the Sun and two balls for the Earth and Moon. Move the Moon round behind the Earth. See how the Earth's shadow gives the Moon its crescent shape.

Earth night

Earth day

Moon in shadow

Lunatic!

The Romans thought that the Moon could affect their minds and that lunatics became madder as the Moon waxed. The word **lunatic** comes from **luna** – which means moon.

Make a sundial

You will need:

Large piece of paper
Stick
4 stones
(A sunny day!)

Push a stick through the centre of the paper

Mark the stick's shadow every hour

Put a large piece of paper on the ground

Hold it in place with 4 stones

You can record what your sundial tells you on this chart.
Use a compass to help you find South.

	10 o'clock	11 o'clock	12 o'clock	1 o'clock	2 o'clock	3 o'clock	4 o'clock
Where is the Sun?							
Where is the shadow?							
Length of shadow							

Here's how we filled in part of our chart.

12 o'clock

It was midday

The Sun was high in the South

The shadow was pointing North

very short — The shadow was very short

Which direction did the Sun seem to move in?

Did the shadow move in the same direction?

Does the shadow move right round the stick? Why not?

Does the shadow change length and why?

Shadow pictures

torch

large pottery mug or vase

You can use lots of different objects. By moving the torch higher or lower, see how the shadow shape alters.

Make a rabbit

Your hand should be much nearer to the wall than the light is.

Can you see an eye?

Can you make the ears move?

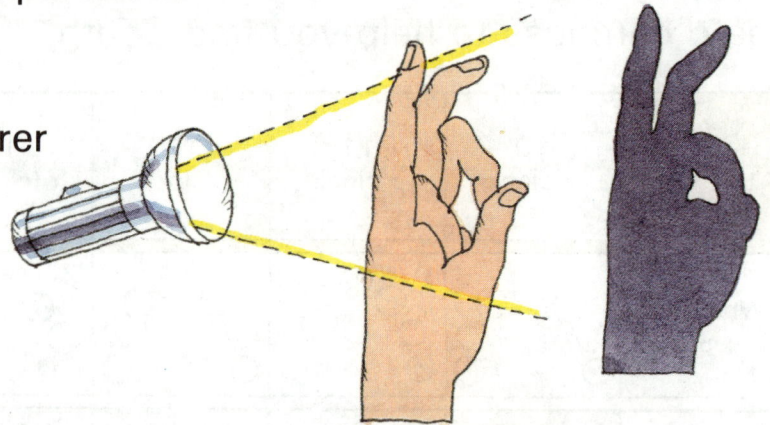

Here's another one to try

Can you guess what it is?

Move your hands to make the wings flap.

Perhaps you can invent some of your own.

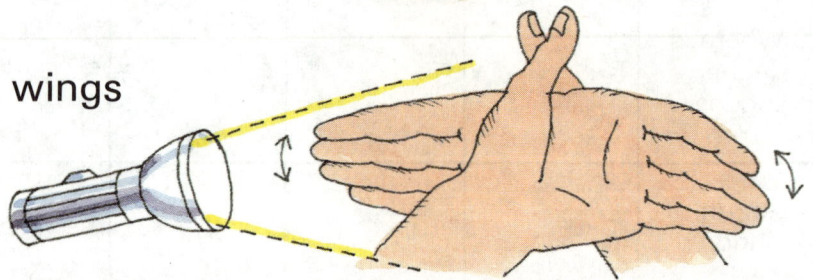

Words you need to know

If light can pass through something, we say it is **translucent**.

If you can actually see through it, like a window, it is **transparent**.

If no light gets through, it is **opaque**.

Match the object to the correct word.

translucent

transparent

opaque

Check the forecast!

Watch the weather forecast on TV for a week.

Were they right?

Days of the week	M	T	W	T	F	S	S
Forecast symbol	☀						
Actual symbol	☀						
Was it right?	yes						

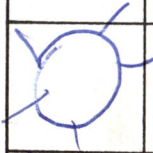

Find the answers

Why does an airport have a windsock?

What is a weather vane?

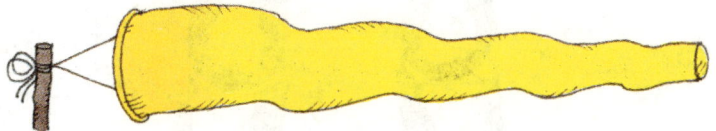

Here are some old sayings about weather. Are they true?

Earthworms come to the surface in damp conditions.

Cattle lie down before rain.

Pigs' tails straighten when rain is near.

Where the rainbow ends is a crock of gold.

A rainbow in the morning is the shepherd's warning,
To carry his coat on his back.
But a rainbow at night is the shepherd's delight,
For then no coat will he lack.

When sheep do huddle by tree and bush,
Bad weather is coming with wind and slush.

YOUR BODY

It all fits!

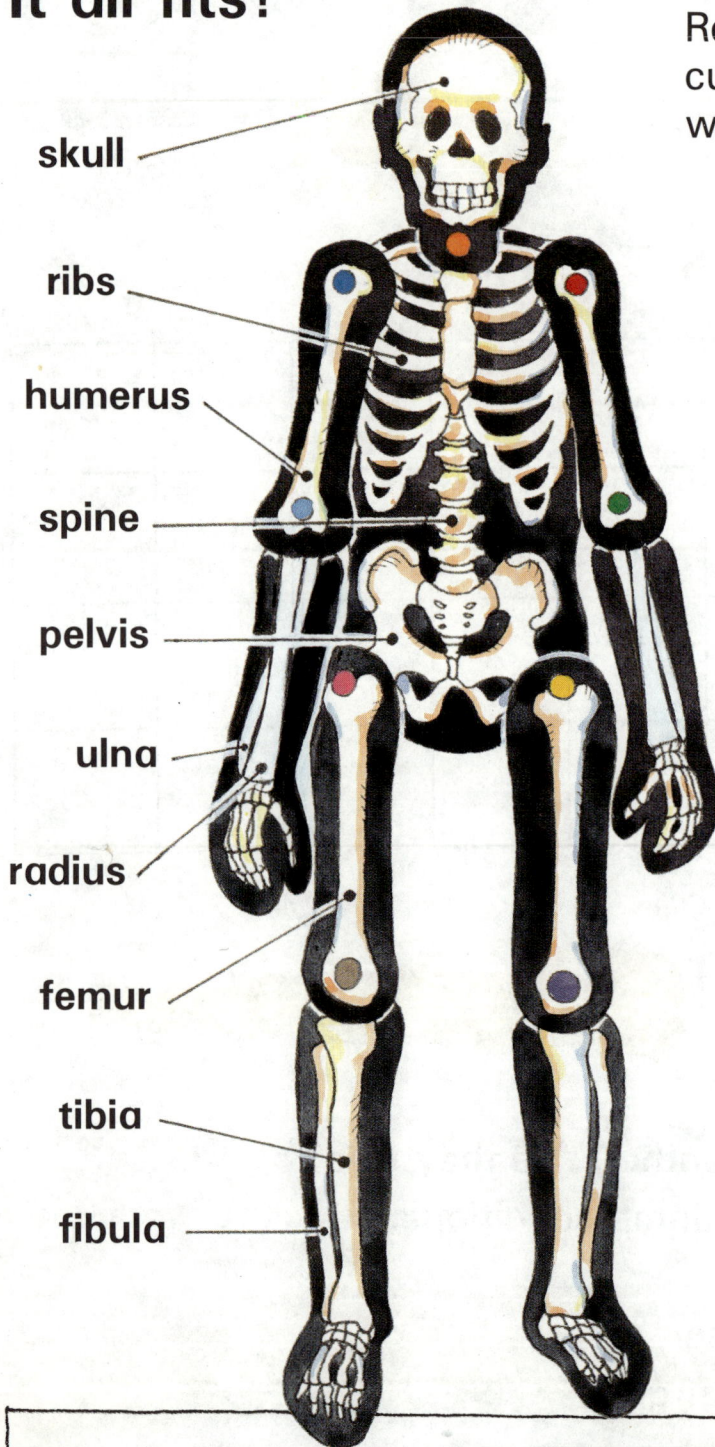

Read this page carefully then cut out the pieces on the card which follows.

Match the colours to get the pieces in the right places.

The inside story!

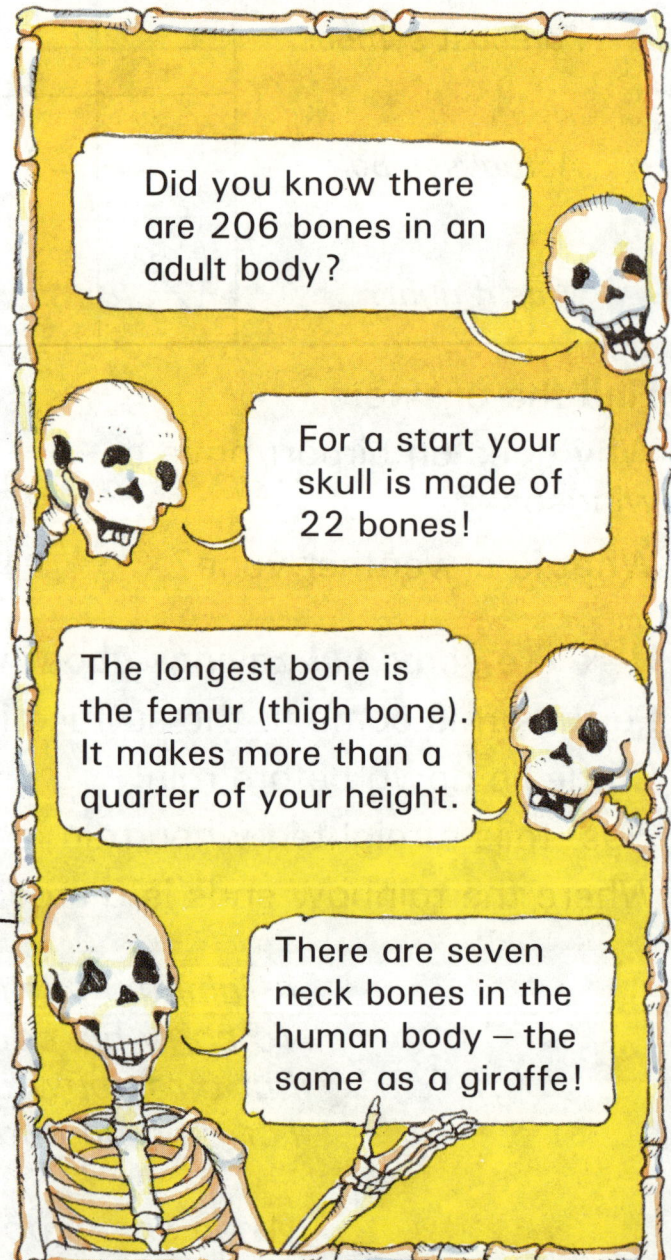

skull

ribs

humerus

spine

pelvis

ulna

radius

femur

tibia

fibula

Use brass paper fasteners so that the joints will move.

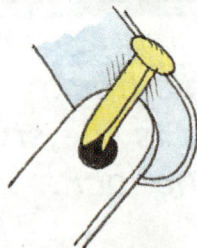

Did you know there are 206 bones in an adult body?

For a start your skull is made of 22 bones!

The longest bone is the femur (thigh bone). It makes more than a quarter of your height.

There are seven neck bones in the human body – the same as a giraffe!

Build yourself a skeleton!

Instructions on previous page.

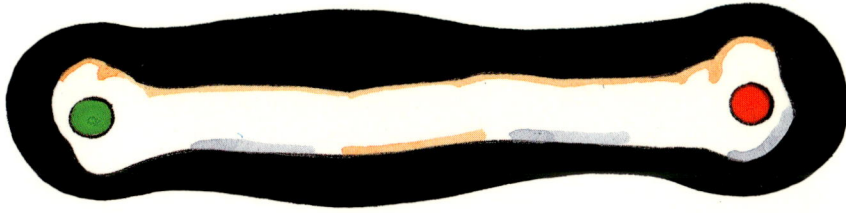

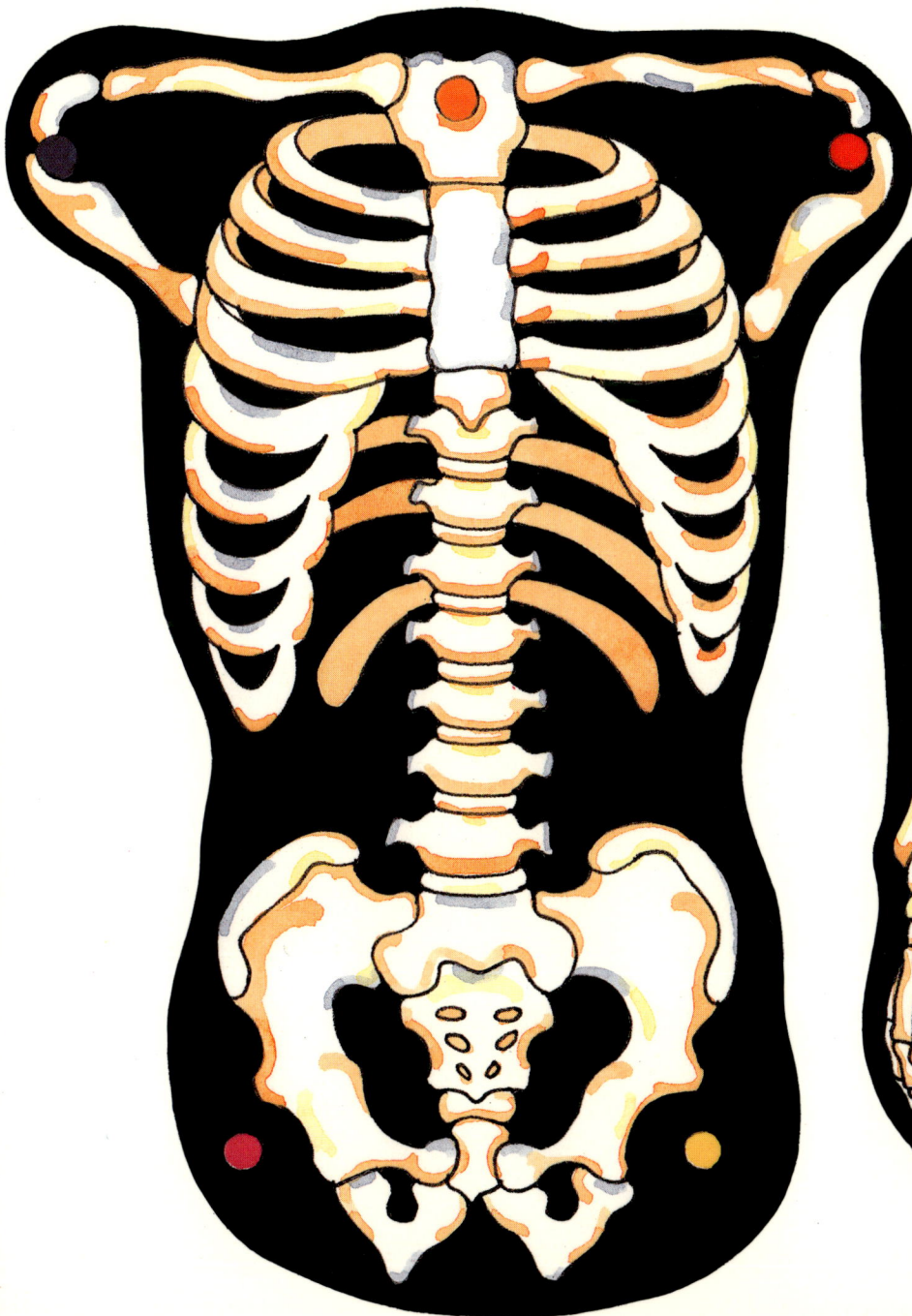

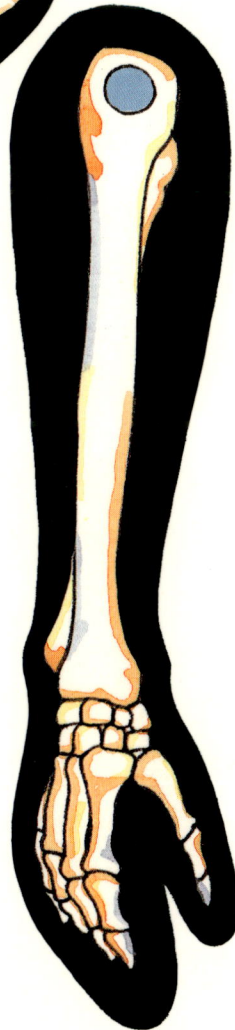

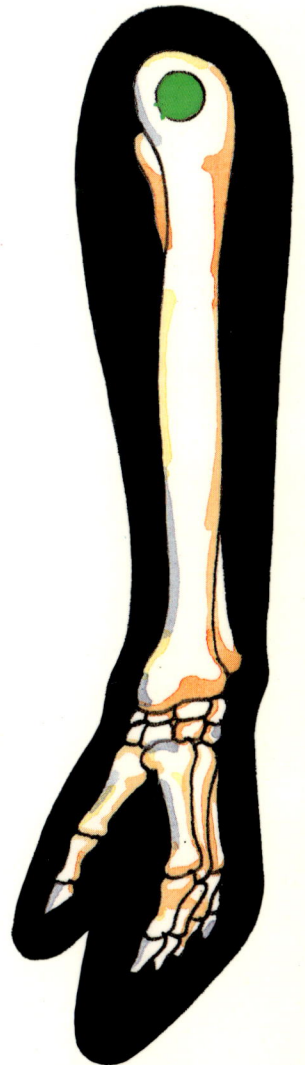

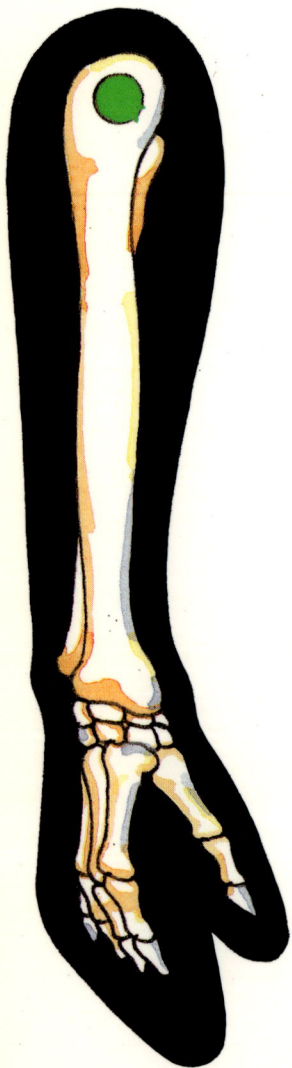

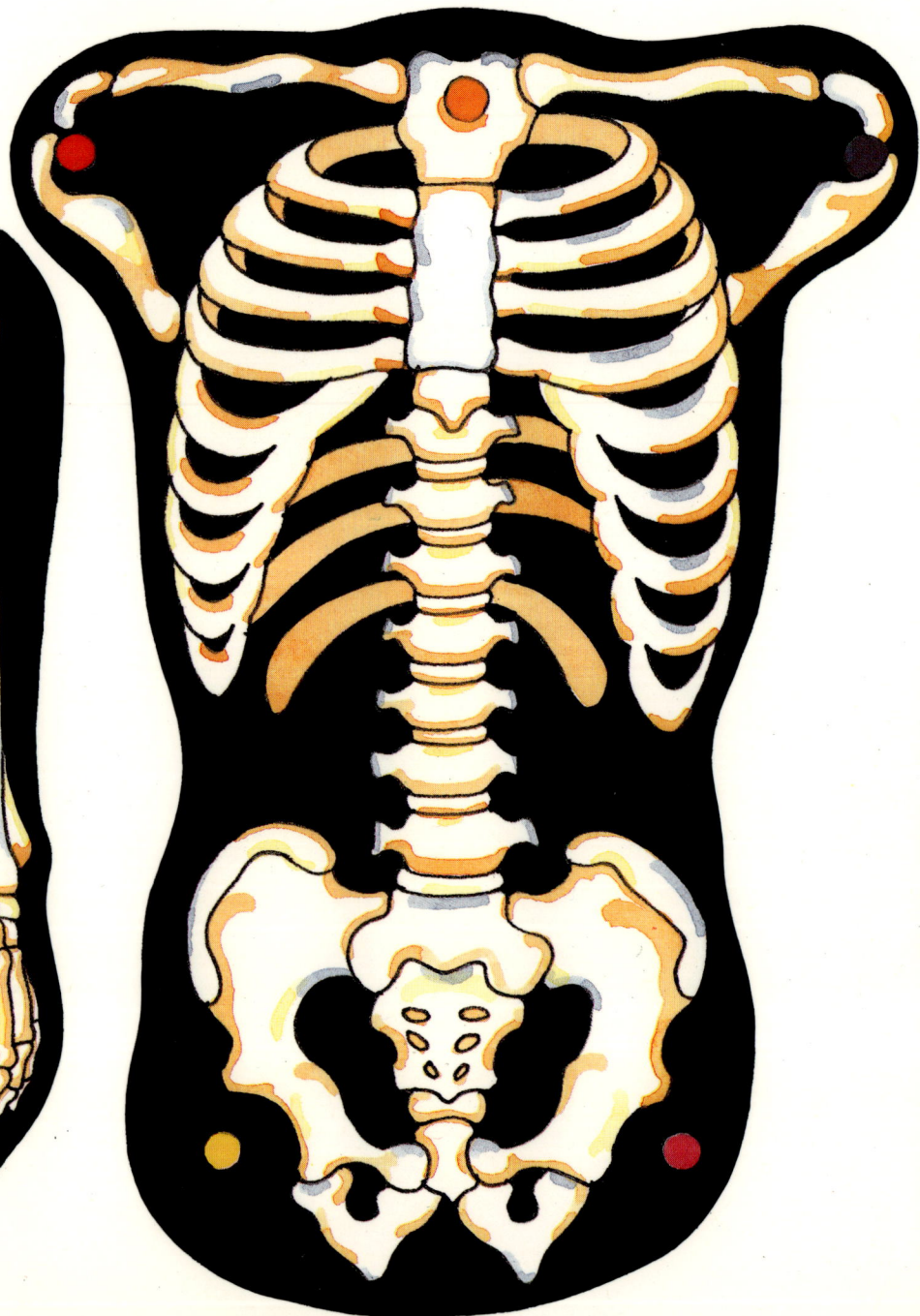

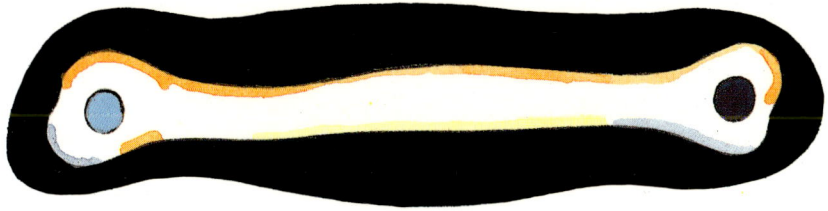

Bones, bones...

Here are the skeletons of some animals you know. Can you tell which is which?

There is a frog, a bat, a penguin, a cat, a fish and a snake.

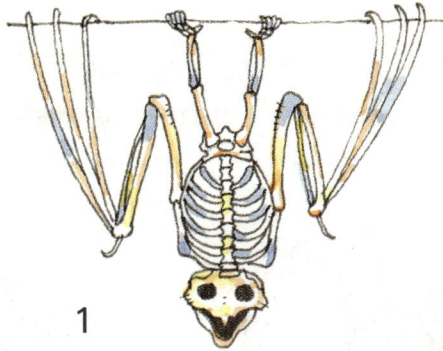

1

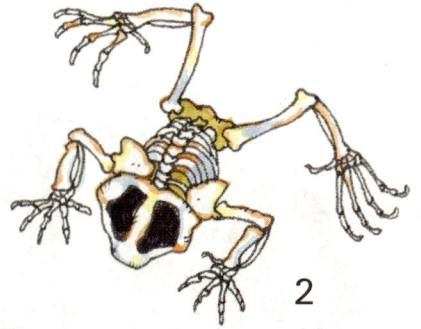

2

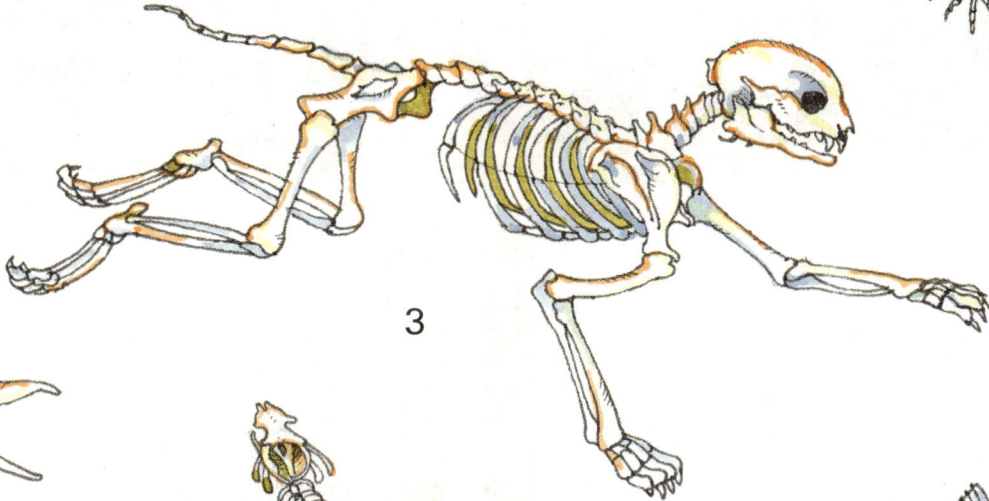

3

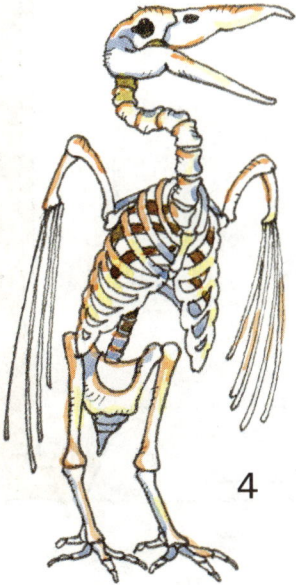

4

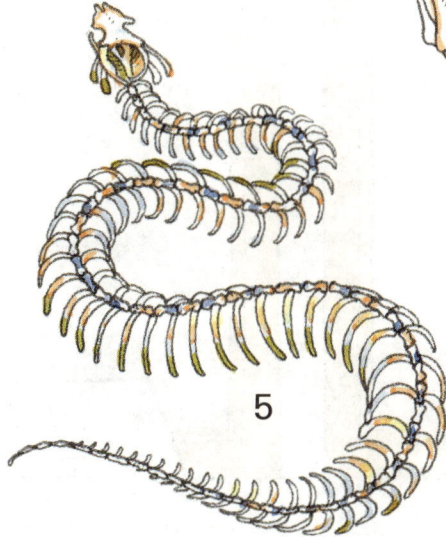

5

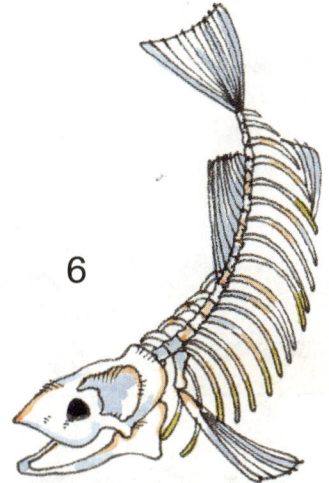

6

Why couldn't the skeleton go to the ball?

Because he'd got **nobody** to go with.

Why couldn't the bones get out of the cupboard?

Because they'd lost the **skeleton** key!

No two alike!

People are different. Look carefully at a friend. What are the differences between you? Sit side by side in front of a mirror and draw your portraits in the boxes below.

me

Now write down these measurements for both of you.

weight _____ _____

height _____ _____

waist _____ _____

head _____ _____

feet _____ _____

hands _____ _____

Test your reflexes

Ask your friend to make a quick movement in front of your eyes.

Be careful not to poke anyone in the eye!

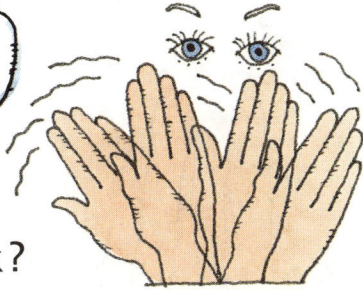

Did you blink?

Give your friend a feather and ask him or her to tickle the back of your neck.

What do you feel?

Sit on a chair and cross your legs. Shut your eyes and ask a friend to tap just below the knee with the side of the hand.

What happens?

How many people in your family are ticklish?

What a blow

Set up this experiment.

large glass jar full of water

plastic tubing going into neck of jar

large bowl full of water

Take a deep breath and blow steadily through the tube for as long as you can. Now look at the jar. You will be able to see how much air was in your lungs.

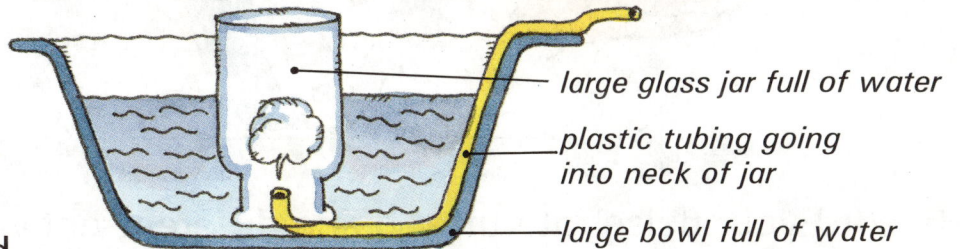

Did you know?

There are some things your body does all by itself. You don't have to think about breathing or keeping your heart beating and you can't NOT blink for very long – try it!

Animals can't control blinking at all. You could outstare a tiger!

Find your pulse

The throb of your pulse is waves of blood travelling from the heart through your body. Here is how to measure your heart beat.

Sit quietly and lay one hand in your lap, palm upwards. With the *fingers* of your other hand you can find the pulse in your wrist. It's along a straight line down from your thumb.

Count how many beats in one minute. ☐

Now jump, run or skip for a few minutes and count the beats again. ☐

Why do you think there's a difference? How long does it take for your **pulse rate** to return to normal? ☐

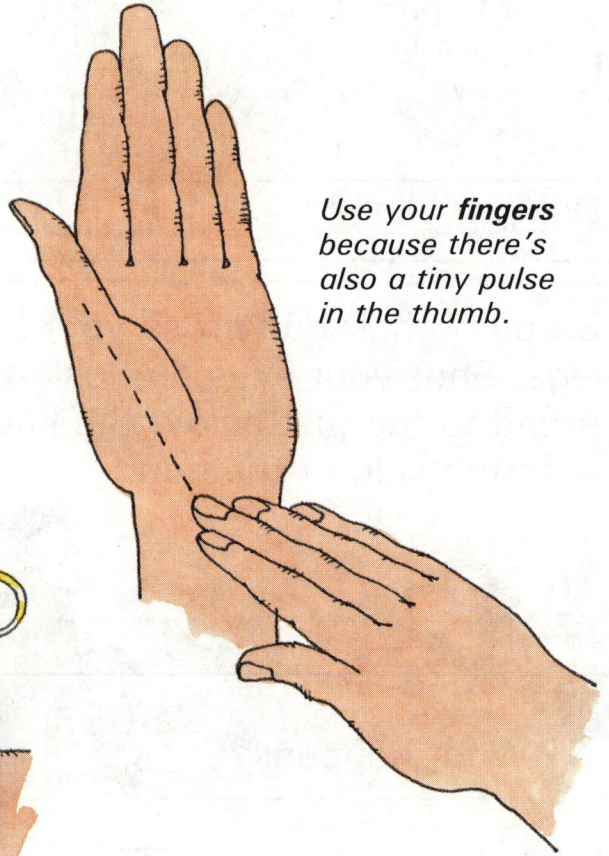

*Use your **fingers** because there's also a tiny pulse in the thumb.*

Record your pulse rate after doing different activities.

☐ ☐

☐ ☐

Did you know your heart beats at about 70 beats every minute? During your whole life your heart could beat 3,000 million times!

Sight

Which eye do you use most?

Hold a pencil upright at arm's length. Line it up with a door or window frame keeping *both* eyes open.

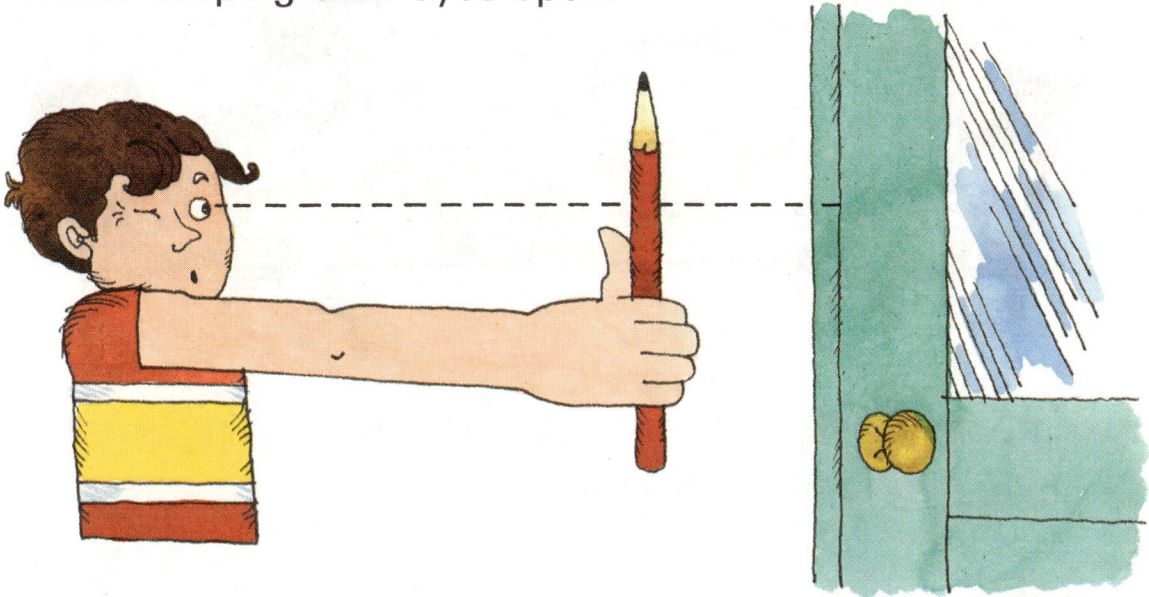

Close your right eye. Open it. Close your left eye. Open it.

The pencil will usually stay lined up with the window frame when you use your **dominant** eye but it will appear to move when you use the other eye.

Your dominant eye is the one you use most.

Watch the pupil

Ask a friend to sit facing the window or a light. Look at the pupil in each eye.

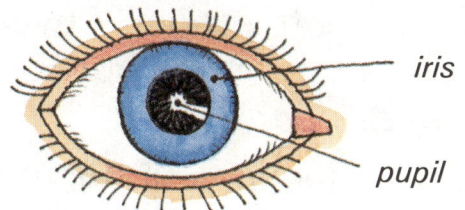

iris

pupil

Now ask him or her to close both eyes and cover them with both hands. Count to 20.

When the eyes are opened again have the pupils changed? Draw the answer.

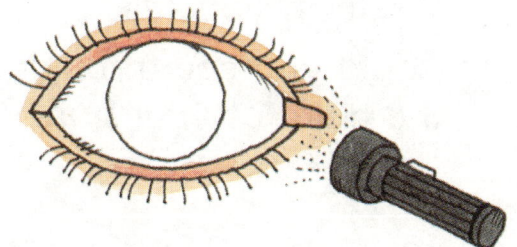

Try shining a torch into your friend's eyes.

Why two eyes?

Ask another person to sit opposite you at a table. Ask them to hold out a pencil, point upwards with the other end resting on the table.

With both eyes *open*, you touch the point with the point of *your* pencil.

Easy!

Now try with one eye closed. This isn't as easy, is it?

You need two eyes to judge distance.

You can test this out on your own by holding a pen at arm's length and putting the top on. Then try with each eye closed.

How strange!

Roll a sheet of paper into a tube. Hold the tube to one eye and look across the room. Cover the other eye with your hand but *still keep both eyes open*.

Now move your hand away from your eye along the side of the tube.

What do you see?

Could you see through the "hole" in the palm of your hand?

Do your eyes deceive you?

These are called **optical illusions**.

Which line is longer? Measure them both!

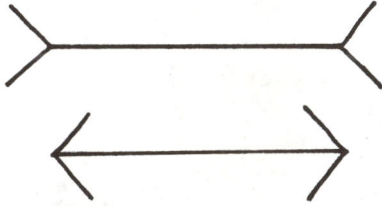

Are the shaded surfaces on the top or bottom of each cube.

Is this hat bigger across its brim or bigger from top to bottom? Measure it!

Which shape is bigger?

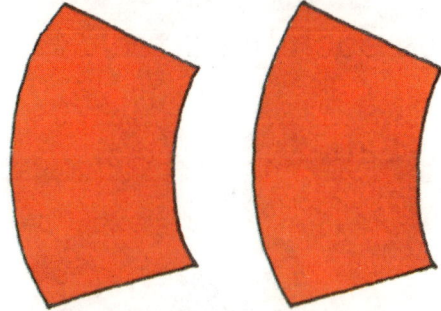

Which white circle is larger?

Can you see two heads or a candlestick?

Is the arrow straight?

Look at the basket and watch the handle change position from side to side!

What has an eye but cannot see?

A needle

Touch

You can tell whether something is hot or cold by touching it. But is this *always* true?

Try this.

Fill three bowls with water.

One hot (not burning hot!) one very cold and one warm.

Put one hand into the hot water and the other into the cold water. Slowly count up to 100. Then put both hands into the warm water.

How does each hand feel?

Left.................................   Right.................................

Touch your throat gently with your fingers and say **aaagh** quite loudly.

What do you feel?

Is there a difference when you say **ssshh**?

Make a list of sounds you can feel in your throat.

Which sounds do you think these faces are making?

TEMPERATURE

A **thermometer** tells us how hot or cold it is.

Try to buy a cheap thermometer mounted on wood from somewhere like a garden centre or hardware shop.

Never put a thermometer in very hot water and never put it in your mouth.

Each mark on the thermometer is one degree Celsius or **1°C**.

Measure the temperature in different places and at different times and keep a chart like this.

	Outside		Fridge		Bedroom		Sunny window	
	am	pm	am	pm	am	pm	am	pm

45
40
35
30
25
20
15
10
5
°C

Did you know?

Your body temperature is usually about 37°C but it may go up or down if you are not well.

Some animals are called cold-blooded. This doesn't mean that their blood is cold but that their body temperature depends on their environment.

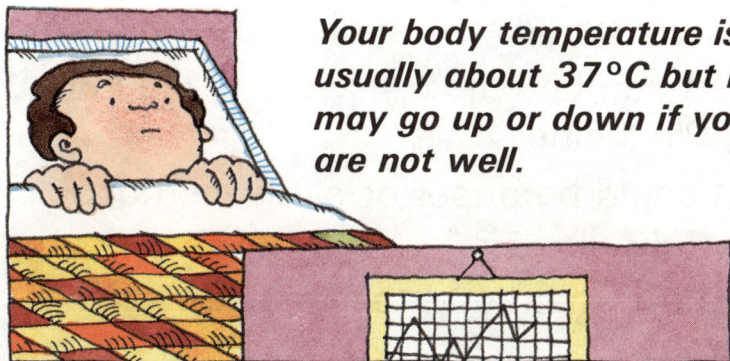

Pushes and pulls

Which car will win?

Try it out. The two cars must be the same. One weight is heavier than the other.

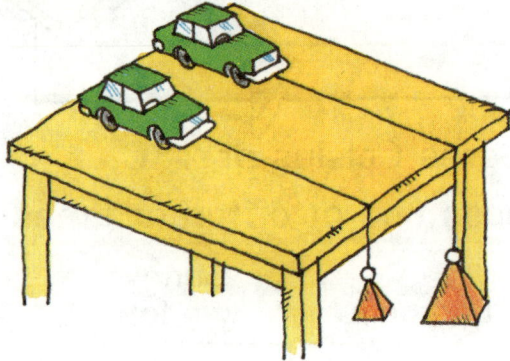

The one with the heaviest weight wins. It has more **force** *pulling* it along.

Which boat goes fastest?

Try it out. The boats must be the same, but one has a bigger sail than the other.

The one with the biggest sail has more **force** *pushing* it along.

Make your own boats

The boats you use for the test can be made of many things. You could use wood scraps, or foil food dishes. You could use plastic trays from supermarkets. You could even make small boats from walnut shells!

How important do you think the shape is?

The mast can be wood or wire, glued in or held by Plasticine.

The sail could be paper or cloth, perhaps even metal foil.

Make lots of them and test to see which is the best.

Air power

Air can apply the **force** to make all sorts of things work.

Here is a hovercraft you can make from a margarine tub and a toilet roll tube. Cut a hole in the tub and cut some flaps on the end of the tube so that you can tape it to the tub. The flaps will hold it firmly in place.

Now blow down the tube and see the tub hover.

Draw a circle on card and then draw a spiral line like this from the middle all the way to the edge.

Cut it out and hang it over a hot radiator. It will spin round. Why do you think it does that?

Why it works

The spiral acts like a propeller, but backwards. The force *comes from hot air rising from the radiator.*

Slow down a bit!

Air doesn't just make things go faster. It can slow them down, too.

Why not make a parachute? This one is made from a handkerchief with thread tied to the corners and then to a heavy weight.

You could try different materials to see which is best. What about tissue paper, or clingfilm? Try different plastic bags, some are thicker than others.

Are four threads enough or does it work better with more?

Give yourself a test

What can you remember?
Look back in the book if you've forgotten.

1   When a battery is wired to a bulb
    so that the bulb lights up, we call this a _____

2   What do we call materials that stop
    some colours of light passing through? _____

3   What's another name for a rainbow? _____
    Do you know which seven
    colours make one of these?_____

    _____

4   Are these statements true or false?
        The Moon orbits the Earth. TRUE/FALSE
        The Sun orbits the Earth. TRUE/FALSE
        The Moon and Earth orbit the Sun. TRUE/FALSE

5   What do we call a surface or
    object where no light can get through? _____

6   Which is the longest bone in your body? _____

7   What do we call the bones in a human or animal body? _____

8   How many bones in an adult human body?_____